The Worship Leader's
MANUAL

A GUIDE TO A HEALTHY AND IMPACTFUL WORSHIP TEAM

Anna Lonelle

COPYRIGHT © 2024 ANNA LONELLE

ALL RIGHTS RESERVED.

ABOUT
me

ABOUT me

Pastor Anna Lonelle Pringle; most popularly known as Anna Lonelle, is an urban gospel artist and a native of Atlanta, GA. Pastor Anna started her career at the early age of 7 and accepted her call to ministry at the age of 14.

God made Anna acutely aware of the greater kingdom work He was calling her to, early in her walk. Anna began to take her passion for unbridled worship and used it to fuel and develop the kingdom weapon that is her voice. Her relationship with God further thrust her towards her passion for kingdom advancement – which led to her being ordained to the pastorate at Embassy International Worship Center in 2017. Anna has released several projects including her first solo album 'Anna Lonelle- Live in Atlanta, Month of Moments by Embassy Worship, Possess The Land by Embassy Worship , and many more projects . She has also sung background vocals for many established Gospel Artist and currently serves as the Worship Pastor for Embassy City Church in Atlanta, Ga under the leadership of Apostle Bryan and Pastor Patrice Meadows. Anna is also a proud mentee of Apostle Psalmist Raine out of Chicago, Illinois.

In 2018, God led Pastor Anna to share her testimony of trial and triumph on her journey to accepting her call, in her first published book "From Glory to Grace: The Story of a Rose" which is available on Amazon.

Pastor Anna is a devoted wife to her husband Robert and together they have a beautiful son, Arrow.

Pastor Anna's voice carries a unique sound that captivates congregations and a vibrant personality that evokes security in the faith of other believers. Pastor Anna's music is both beautifully orchestrated and prophetically positioned to shift the atmosphere wherever it is released and unravels generational bondage off God's people.
She has found passion in developing worship leader's from all over the world through her mentorship group " Worship Leader's Unite" and has created training and development tracts for worship leaders and their teams.

OVERVIEW

How to build a team you can trust
- Auditions
- Interviews
- Contracts
- Laying out your expectations
- Probationary period

How to build a set list
- The sound of the house
- Establishing a Sound
- Picking songs based on themes
- Honoring the history of the church

How to make room for a star
- How to give opportunities to gifted people
- How to deal with jealousy and feelings of insecurity

How to build a relationship with your music director
- Learning when to speak up and when to stay in your lane
- Building a relationship outside of ministry
- Creating a safe place for honesty
- The fine line between macroo-managment and abandonment
- Preparation is key

How to train your team
- Spiritual Training
- How to assess areas of growth
- How to prepare a training for your team

OVERVIEW

How to please God and your Pastor

- Building relationship/Trust with your Pastor
- Handling disagreements/differences of opinions
- How to undergird the vision your pastor has for the team
- When you are forced to choose, choose God; honorably.

How to handle loss

- Don't take it personal
- Assess the reason for the loss
- Assess the temperature of your team

Worship Leader vs. Worship Pastor

- The differences in expectations and spiritual

How to balance ministry and your personal life

- Self care
- Scheduling time off (Will the church survive without you?)
- Getting poured into for yourself
- Should I get a mentor?

The humanity of a Worship Leader

- The glory after the fall
- Restoration and forgiveness

INTRODUCTION

This book is dedicated to every worship leader around the world who desires to grow a healthy and impactful team. Some of you were thrust into this position without training, resources, or support. Well, I pray that this manual gives you some of the tools you'll need to leave an imprint on your team. Thank you for your "YES!" You are needed and necessary and the health of your team depends on the health of its leader! This step towards developing yourself is already a step in the right direction. You are entering a judgment-free zone where you are officially allowed to be honest and vulnerable. Take this time to examine yourself and your team and see what you can implement into your team's culture.

CHAPTER one

How to build a Team you can trust

Holding auditions for a worship team is essential to ensure that team members are not only musically skilled but also aligned with the spiritual mission of the worship experience. Here's a brief guide on how to do it effectively:

Preparation:

Set clear expectations: Define the roles you're auditioning for (altos, sopranos, tenors) In some seasons you may only be looking for sopranos. Make it clear in your promo video, flyer, or announcements what you are specifically looking for.

Choose a location: Ensure the audition space is conducive to hearing the nuances of each singer and private enough to ask important questions during their interview. (Rehearsal room or office space)

Select audition pieces: Choose songs that are common in your worship repertoire. Tell them which song to sing, do not allow them to adjust the key. We want to hear their range and ability to sing their part(sop,alt,ten)in the original key of the song.

Promotion:

Advertise: Use church announcements,social media, and word of mouth to promote the auditions.

Schedule: Determine if auditions will be one on one or with a group. Set your auditions at a specific time.

CHAPTER one
Cont'd

Pay attention to their punctuality; if they are late for auditions, they will likely be late for rehearsal and soundcheck.

The Audition:

Warm welcome: Ensure that the environment is welcoming, and help to ease any nerves.

Audition form: Have each participant fill out a form providing details about their musical experience, spiritual journey, and personal information.

Performance: Allow each person to perform the assigned piece.

Feedback: Give constructive feedback, and allow them to sing a portion of the song again. If they are able to make the adjustment, it shows they are teachable. If they struggle to make the correction, it could be a sign of trouble ahead.

Spiritual Alignment:

Interview: Engage them in a conversation about their faith journey, understanding of worship, and reasons for joining the team. Ensure that they have been a member of the church for at least 3-6 months before auditioning. Requiring them to take a new members class is also a great way to ensure that they understand the vision of the house and the biblical foundation of your church. Through this process you can determine if they are a babe in Christ, a mature believer, or currently struggling in their christian walk.

Bring a Camera and a Witness: Recording each audition allows you to go back and assess the audition. It gives you time to weigh your decision. You should also bring a witness, specifically someone from your team who already serves with you to weigh in on the decision. This person can respectfully give their opinion on whether or not they believe this candidate would gel well and be an asset to the team. You can also use this team member to sing with the new candidate to assess their musical ability further.

CHAPTER ONE
Cont'd

Post-Audition:

Decision-making: Review all the auditions with other core teammates, considering both musical skill and spiritual maturity. As the leader you must make the final decision.

Communication: Promptly inform auditionees of your decision, whether they have made the team or not. You can do so via email. Include their audition video in the email.

Feedback: Offer feedback and areas of improvement for those who didn't make it. Encourage them to audition again in the future.

Integration:

Orientation: For those who are selected, provide an orientation that covers team expectations, schedules, and any other essential information.

Probationary Period: Once they have made the team, place them on a 60 day probation. Even though they auditioned and made the team, this will ensure that you made the right decision. Observe how they get along with the team, watch their punctuality, and watch how they keep up musically,spiritually with the rest of the team.

Rehearsals: Incorporate them into regular rehearsals as soon as possible. Have them sit in rehearsal even when they are not scheduled to sing so they can get accustomed to how you run rehearsal.

Remember, while musical talent is important, the heart and spirit behind the worship are paramount. Always consider both aspects when selecting team members.

CHAPTER ONE
Cont'd

When introducing a new team member, it is important to make them feel welcome by organizing a small party. Include all team members in the celebration to help them get acquainted with the new addition. This can be as simple as ordering a small cake, balloons, and a card with a special note from the team. Such gestures will facilitate the transition for both the new member and the existing team.

Building trust takes time. It requires leaders to relinquish control, which can be challenging. However, it is crucial for effective leadership. Here are a few ways to build trust with your team:

1. **Lead by Example:**
Demonstrate trustworthiness through your actions. Be reliable, honest, and transparent in your interactions with team members.
Show a strong work ethic and commitment to the team's goals. When your team sees your dedication, they are more likely to reciprocate.

2. **Effective Communication:**
Encourage open and honest communication. Create an environment where team members feel comfortable expressing their thoughts and ideas with respect and sensitivity.
Listen actively to your team members. Understand their perspectives and show empathy. Responding to their concerns or feedback demonstrates that their voices are heard and valued.

As a leader, I never ask my team members to do anything I wouldn't do myself. I served my season in the background serving many other worship leaders with a pure heart; to the best of my ability. I don't know if there is a humble way to say it but I can honestly say that I would want someone like me on my team. I have always been punctual, prepared with my music, spiritually sensitive, and held down the bgvs with high energy and a positive attitude. I wasn't perfect at all, but I loved serving in the background and that translated through my service. That is why I can demand it from my team. But even in my leadership position, I am aware that my team is watching me. Watching to see if I fast when the church calls a corporate fast. Watching to see if I live the life I sing about, watching to see how I worship through life's many storms. So I have an obligation to lead by example. I may not always get it right, but even in my failures they are watching to see how I pick myself up and recover.

CHAPTER one
Cont'd

Invest in Relationships:

Take the time to get to know your team members on a personal level. Building personal connections helps to create a more supportive and understanding team environment. When I understand the everyday life-load of my teammates I am able to have compassion, give grace, and provide tailored correction when needed.

Tailored correction means that everyone receives the same correction in a different way. Though it is crucial to be fair and unbiased in your treatment of your team, you must also have a personal understanding of your team members so you can be sensitive in how you correct them. For example, Mary and Tim are members of your team and they have to commute an hour from their jobs to the church. Due to traffic, they often find themselves running late. When you auditioned them, you asked if the call time would be a problem and they said "no!" However since they officially joined the team, they have struggled with punctuality. While getting to know Mary, you discover that she was once in a verbally and physically abusive relationship for five years. So although you must correct her and challenge her to honor the expectations and commitment she made, when you speak to her you will do so with sensitivity, compassion, and firmness. On the other hand, Tim may be able to handle a more direct approach. Once again, with both team members you must be honest and firm but you will have to use wisdom with each member to understand them and then address any conflict accordingly.

Organize team-building activities or events outside of regular rehearsals to strengthen the bonds among team members. Fellowship with your team is just as important as bible study. The teams relationship will translate on stage. The worship experience is powerful when you actually love the people you serve alongside. Fasting and praying together is necessary but so is breaking bread together.

CHAPTER one
Cont'd

What are some important qualities that you are looking for in your team?

List some ways to bring those qualities out of your team.

_____
_____
_____
_____
_____
_____
_____
_____
_____
_____
_____
_____
_____
_____
_____
_____
_____

Chapter One Cont'd

CHAPTER TWO

How to build a set list

The Sound of The House

Every church has a distinctive sound, much like our unique thumbprint. The sound of your church is a crucial part of it's established culture. It is very important that you grab hold and embrace your sound and remain consistent. This means that you must fully embrace the fact that not every hot new song on the radio is suitable for your church. As a worship leader you need to separate the songs that you listen to for your own enjoyment from the songs that you add to your setlist and release over your congregation. As worship leaders we are gatekeepers, which means we must be good stewards of what is released through the worship experience.

If you have inherited the worship leader position, be sensitive to the history of the sound of the house. If you are new be careful to honor the established sound of the house while also seeking God's direction concerning what he desires to do next through you. If you are a first generation worship leader at your church, you have the opportunity to establish the sound. Allow your pastor to cast vision and share what his vision is for the sound of the house.

Things you can consider when establishing the sound;

Denomination, Age range of the congregation, the personality of the senior leaders, the current spiritual climate and more.

Take a second and imagine you are at Pastor Joel Olsteen's church and for worship they have Ricky Dillard come out with his choir and sing "Best Day of My Life". I can imagine the confusion and awkwardness of the congregation. Two amazing ministries and ministry gifts with two different sounds and cultures. I do want to make clear that this is not a race thing, though race can play a factor in the culture of the church. There are gifts from different backgrounds that fit the sound of the house regardless of age, race, and other barriers. For example David and Nicole Binion have successfully cultivated a sound that crosses over and bridges the gap between many different social and ethnicity borders. The same can be said for Cee Cee Winans. She has won over a large demographic of believers. This is less about cultivating a sound that is acceptable in all arenas and more about how you should stay true to the identity that God gave you. You must embrace the fact that your expression may not be for everyone.

Chapter Two Cont'd

How to build a set list

As a prophetic-apostolic worship leader, I understand that my demonstrative, roaring, and authoritative expression of worship may not be everyone's cup of tea, but my assignment remains the same. So spend time with God and ask Him for direction and wisdom on how to minister a song and which songs to include in your setlist. Additionally, before sending the music off to your team, send it to your pastor and ask him is this the direction he would like to go during worship. This may be something that you do in the infancy of your worship ministry. As time goes on, trust will be established and you will no longer have to send in the setlist. He will trust that you now understand the vision and sound of the house. Though micromanagement can be a sign of distrust, shift your perspective, remain positive, and allow him to give his input earlier on in the development phase of the team. You will appreciate the foundation of the relationship that is being established. This relationship will come in handy in the future when you need to discuss different matters concerning the team.

Now that you have had time to think about the sound of your house, let's discuss how to create a set-list. Choosing songs to sing can be a tedious and sometimes frustrating process. Let me teach you a formula I use to build a dynamic setlist. First build a catalog of all of the songs your team has ever sung. Separate them by categories. (uptempo praise songs, mid tempo, slow worship songs) You can even include the key of each song beside the title. To help you tell a cohesive story or convey a consistent message, write the theme of each song beside it.

CHAPTER Two
Cont'd

How to build a set list

Example: Made A Way - Travis Greene Bm (Theme: Faith and Hope) (Mid tempo song)

Once you have established a catalog of all your songs, try to find out what your pastor is preaching about. What is the current series your pastor is in? Imagine that for a month, your pastor will be teaching on a series called "Jesus is King". In the series he is preaching about how we need to exalt God in everything that we do. Now that I know the theme I am going to pray and ask the Lord to highlight which songs emphasize the message my pastor is already preaching about. Some songs that may pop up are "Name above all names" by Eddie James, or "Your Great Name" by Todd Dulaney, or "The Name of Jesus Lifted High" by Eddie James. As you get into a rhythm, this should become easier for you. The reality is that you may not be able to do this for every single Sunday and Wednesday of the week. Not all of your songs will match your pastor's message but you can make sure that your set for that day has a cohesive message.

Let's discuss the two fast songs and one slow song standard that most American churches have adopted. Though I am not sure of its origin, I can imagine the goal is to build people up in a time of praise and exaltation before slowing things down for a time of intimate worship. I am fully aware of the scripture "we enter into his gates with thanksgiving and into his courts with praise" (Psalms 100:4) but who is to say that giving thanks has to be uptempo? I only want to challenge how we facilitate our worship experiences. There is nothing wrong with the way that it is, but I want us as worship leaders to not be afraid to break tradition if the Lord desires for us to start differently. What if before the band played a note the dancers began to dance to silence, and then the singers joined in, and then the band followed? What would happen if we started off worship with a slow hymn? Have we become religious in our approach?

CHAPTER Two *Cont'd*

Take a moment below and describe the sound of your house.
What is the demographic of your congregation?
What are some songs that fit the sound of your house?

_____
_____
_____
_____
_____
_____
_____
_____
_____
_____
_____
_____
_____
_____
_____

CHAPTER Two Cont'd

CHAPTER Two Cont'd

CHAPTER Three

How To Support A Star On Your Team

Though you may be the worship leader of your team, it is highly likely that there are other incredibly gifted individuals on your team. These individuals may have even led worship at their previous church. They will demonstrate they have more experience than your average teammate. Despite their experience, they have chosen to leave their old church and serve in whatever capacity needed in this current season at this particular local assembly. So as the worship leader, how do you steward them? How can you acknowledge their special gifting and give them space to serve in a greater capacity? What are some challenges around this special circumstance?

Here is a list of reasons why you may struggle to give them opportunities, or know what to do with them.

1. Though they led at their previous church, they have yet to understand the culture, sound of the house, or how to navigate at this house.

At their previous church they were a star! They may have been impactful at their past church. They understood the laws that governed that kingdom. However, now they must familiarize themselves with the identity of this new church. It's similar to a manager from Longhorns having to learn the ways of Ruth Chris. They cannot come from one restaurant to another assuming that it is a "one size fits all" position. What worked there may not work here.

2. They may be unsubmitted and unteachable. Due to their past experience they don't believe you have anything to teach them. Therefore, this can result in a spirit of dishonor.

Learning the laws of honor is an essential when transitioning from one church to another, especially if there is already a worship leader in place. Honor is not a curse word, nor is it a negative concept, honor is an automatic door opener. Honor is a key. Honor grants access where you would typically be denied. I would rather promote an individual with less skill that is teachable than an individual that has all of the experience and is dishonorable.

CHAPTER Three
Cont'd

3. The church does not have the budget to afford more worship leaders on their payroll.

There are some situations that are beyond your control. You may have someone else who could potentially co-lead with you but the church is currently unable to bring anyone else on at the moment. It is important to have an honest conversation with them. Explain the circumstance and give them the opportunity to assist you on a volunteer basis. Make sure they understand the expectations and are committed to serving in this capacity. During this volunteer period, you will have the opportunity to observe how they handle the responsibilities given to them.

4. You struggle with insecurity and fear the long term repercussions of your decision.

Let's be honest, these are real feelings that we all experience in various aspects of our lives. Feeling afraid is nothing to feel ashamed of, but it does indicate a lack of complete trust in God. Some of your fears may be, "Well are they(leadership/the congregation) going to just discard me once they fall in love with the new shiny penny?" or "What if the new worship leader and I don't get along? Will they respect me and appreciate the opportunity I gave them?", "Will they try to take over and completely disregard the foundation I have established?"

If you want to go fast go alone. If you want to go far go together. Unlike a bass guitar where you have the ability to change out the strings when they are dull, or even purchase a new bass. You only get one set of vocal chords. If you have strong individuals on your team, train them up and use them! This will allow you time to rest and recover. Evaluate their motives, heart posture, and make sure they understand your vision, your pastor's vision and heart, and then utilize them. Territorial-ism doesn't work in ministry. If God opened the door for you, no man can shut that door. However, if you sabotage someone else's opportunity to lead worship and walk in their calling, God is displeased.

CHAPTER Three
Cont'd

How have you dealt with gifted people on your team? What are some ways you can create opportunities for them to serve in a greater capacity?

_____
_____
_____
_____
_____
_____
_____
_____
_____
_____
_____
_____
_____
_____
_____
_____
_____

CHAPTER Three
Cont'd

CHAPTER Three
Cont'd

CHAPTER *four*

How To Build a Relationship with Your Music Director:

The relationship you have with your MD is one of the most important relationships you can have as a worship leader. The Music Director has a significant impact on the worship experience. They help establish the sound of the house and ensure that the entire band is working together to produce a seamless worship set through their musical gifts. The MD must be able to pull out the best performance from each instrument contributing to the unified band. Having a healthy relationship with this individual will foster an atmosphere of collaboration, honesty, and creativity.

1. Learning When to Speak Up and When to Stay in Your Lane

- **Self-awareness**: Before expressing a concern or making a suggestion, consider the impact of your words on the overall team dynamics and the project at hand. You are the worship leader and they are the music director. Stay in your lane. There are some things that they will know that you don't and that is okay. Especially if your educational background is not in music. However, don't be discouraged because your voice still matters and holds weight! Learn how to articulate your concerns with respect to their expertise and experience. Though, you should challenge yourself to study this field more so that you can speak with confidence.

- **Small Foxes Spoil The Vine**: Most issues are worth addressing. Letting problems slide due to fear of conflict will establish an atmosphere of tension, offense, and reoccurring issues.. Though you should address concerns that arise, you can always do so with love, compassion, and an open ear to hear their perspective.

- **Timing**: Choose the right time and setting to voice your concerns or suggestions. It's usually more effective to address issues privately rather than in front of the whole team.

CHAPTER four Cont'd

2. Building Relationship Outside of Ministry

- Casual Outings: Invite your music director for coffee or lunch. Casual settings can help both of you get to know each other beyond the work environment.

- Open Communication: Take an interest in their life outside of ministry. Asking simple questions about their weekend or family can open the door to deeper conversations. This will also show them that you care about them beyond their musical contribution to the church.

Celebration and Honor: Take the time to honor them on special holidays. Buy them a cake on their birthday. Plan random times throughout the year to honor them in front of the entire team. Have a gift card or flowers to show your appreciation for all that they do for the team.

3. Creating A Safe Space for Honesty

Open Door Policy: Make it known that you are always open to feedback and encourage your music director to do the same. They should have the freedom to honorably express their concerns and give ideas on things they would like to see changed.

Non-Judgmental Attitude: When having difficult conversations, approach them without preconceived notions or judgments.

Confidentiality: Ensure that private discussions remain private. This will build trust over time.

Embrace Feedback: Show that you value and appreciate feedback by acting on it and making necessary changes.

Chapter Four *Cont'd*

4. A Fine Line Between Macro-management and Abandonment

I know that you trust your music director which may lead you to have a hands-off approach to your leadership style. Though trust is an important component to the relationship dynamic, so is evaluation and vision casting. Even though they lead the band you must still have a relationship with the rest of the band, provide direction, offer support, and give feedback on things you would like to see implemented in the band. For instances, you can schedule monthly meetings with your MD and challenge them to incorporate training, fellowships, bible studies, and set goals for their team.

Here are some strategies to strike a balance between delegation and trust:

- Delegation with Trust: Trust your leaders to handle their responsibilities. Equip them with the necessary tools and resources, and let them take ownership.
- Regular Check-ins: Instead of constant oversight, schedule regular check-ins to discuss progress, challenges, and needs.
- Empower and Support: Offer guidance and resources without overpowering. A leader's role is to nurture and grow their team.

Establishing a relationship with your music director, like any relationship, requires time, effort, and understanding. Prioritize open communication, trust, and mutual respect to foster a healthy and productive partnership.

CHAPTER four
Cont'd

Check the boxes below when tasks have been completed

- ☐ Schedule Lunch with your Music Director

- ☐ Give your Music Director a gift card to show appreciation. Find a way to honor them publicly.

- ☐ Pray for your Music Director and Band

- ☐ Sit down with your Music Director and collaborate on the vision of the worship experience

- ☐ Affirm their creative contribution

- ☐ Address any conflict that you may have with compassion and honesty

CHAPTER five

How To Train Your Team

In this chapter, we will discuss the importance of training your worship team. I want to start by acknowledging that, despite my years of experience, I had unexplainable fear and anxiety surrounding training. Training my team would force me to sit down and assess how I lead worship, why I lead worship, and what processes and tools helped me to be effective in leading worship. It required me to assess myself and then break down the essential information in a way that others could grasp and grow from. Although people expressed a desire to learn how to lead worship, I doubted my ability to break it down and articulate it effectively. It was never about being selfish or wanting to hide the ingredients in the secret sauce. It was me, not believing in me getting in the way. The day you stop being a student is the day you put an expiration date on your ability to be a teacher.

So one day I finally silenced the negative voices in my head and asked God to give me direction on how to break it down for those that desired to walk this path. And God did it! One lesson at a time. God began to download what he desired for me to pour into them. So, fellow worship leader, if you are afraid to train your team, do it anyway! Push past your fear and anxiety and recognize that the growth and strength of your team depend on your ability to cultivate them through training. If you want a strong army, you must teach them how to fight! If you want an impactful team, you must equip them with the tools to be effective in their assignments.

CHAPTER five Cont'd

How To Train Your Team

Here is a good place to start: schedule a day of training for your team. But before you do, assess areas that need attention in your team. For example, you may have a strong group of singers who are vocally skilled but they lack spiritual awareness. They lack sensitivity and pursuit for a move of God. So instead of doing vocal training, do a teaching on how to deepen your relationship with God. Spend time giving them tools on how to hear the voice of God during the worship encounter and in their personal time. Give them scriptures about developing intimacy with God.

Training is not only beneficial for the team's development, but it is also necessary for the church's advancement as well. Your ability to raise up strong leaders ensures the longevity and health of the church. This means that long after you transition out of the position there will be someone in place that has the DNA of the house. If mom refuses to pass down the family recipes they will die with her. We don't want that to be said about the sound and identity of the worship team.

Chapter Five Cont'd

How To Train Your Team

When you are ready to train your team make sure you allocate at least an hour and a half or more to train. You should begin every session with a teaching and then the second half should be hands-on training. This is also a great time to do some spiritual impartation for the team, for example taking your entire worship team through a private deliverance session or bringing someone in to pour into them on a deeper spiritual level to realign and reunify the team. If they are constantly pouring out week to week, when do they get a chance to be refilled?

You can even hire a vocal coach to hone in on some areas of weakness on the team. You can build a strong army if you no longer ignore the problem and begin to come up with a strategy to strengthen the team in every way. Another powerful muscle to build is unity! Spending time building relationships is just as important as reading the word of God. Carve out time to fellowship with your team and you will see a major impact while you worship together on stage. My ability to look back at my team and genuinely smile because we have an authentic relationship and I trust them, is something that I don't take for granted.

CHAPTER *five* Cont'd

What are some better ways that you can train and develop your team. List below a few areas that you would like to focus on.

_____
_____
_____
_____
_____
_____
_____
_____
_____
_____
_____
_____
_____
_____

CHAPTER five
Cont'd

CHAPTER five
Cont'd

CHAPTER SIX

How to Please God and Your Pastor

If your pastor is anything like mine, you have a leader who is heavily invested in the worship culture of the church. Here are a few common things your pastor may expect from the worship team:

They care about the quality, spiritual maturity, and sanctity of the worship team. Quality meaning, they want us to be a group of vocally strong and skilled singers. Spiritual maturity meaning, that they want to ensure that the team has a clear understanding of "why" we worship and "who" we are worshiping. Lastly, they want to ensure that we are living lives that are pure and fully represent the songs we sing about. They want us to lead by example in our lifestyle and attitude.

Listed below are some ways to better support your pastor and handle challenges that may arise:

1. Building a Relationship and Trust with Your Pastor:
Open Communication: Engage in regular dialogue with your pastor. Seek opportunities to share your thoughts, feelings, and questions. This will build trust over time.

Actively listen when your pastor speaks, listen intently. Make sure you understand their perspective, vision, and the message they are trying to convey.

Understand that having access to your pastor is an honor and privilege. Don't waste their time. Before you meet with your pastor, write a list of important questions you have for him concerning your worship team. Ask him to give you feedback on what he has observed from the worship experience so far.

CHAPTER Six
Cont'd

2. Learn How to Handle Disagreements and Differences of Opinions:

Stay Calm: When disagreements arise, maintain your composure. Maintain a spirit of Honor. Approach the conflict with a sober heart and a desire to understand.

Empathetic Approach: Put yourself in your pastor's shoes. Understand the burden of their responsibility and the reason behind their decisions.

Seek Private Discussion: If you have concerns or disagreements, it's often best to discuss them privately rather than in a public or group setting.

Agree to Disagree: Remember that it's okay to have differences in opinions. What's essential is the bond of unity in the body of Christ.

3. Learn How to Effectively Undergird the Vision Your Pastor Has For the Team:

When it comes to the worship team we must remember that their opinion matters. They may not be able to do what you do, but they can tell you what their vision is for the team and it is your job to yield to that instruction and produce. Here are a few things you must do:

Embrace the Vision: First and foremost, try to understand and internalize the vision your pastor has shared. Reflect on its purpose and relevance.

Support in Action: After your pastor has "written the vision and made it plain" it's time to get to work. There is a funny meme that says "When your wife says" when you get a chance" just go ahead and put your shoes on. She means now" The same applies for our leadership. When they make a suggestion, we should move with intention to get it done and honor their idea.

Share the Vision: Motivate and encourage your team members to align with the vision. Share the benefits and the bigger picture with them.

Provide Constructive Feedback: If you believe there are areas of improvement in the vision or its execution, share your feedback respectfully and offer potential solutions

CHAPTER Six
Cont'd

4. Find Peace in Knowing That You May Not be Able to Please Both:

Seek Godly Wisdom: When in doubt, seek God's guidance. Through prayer and scripture, ask Him to guide your decisions.

Honor God in your Choices: If faced with a situation where you have to choose between pleasing God and Man, always choose God. Do this with respect, humility, and grace.

Have an Open Conversation with Your Pastor: If you feel that following God's direction might not align with your pastor's wishes, have an open conversation with them. Share your feelings and concerns, ensuring you communicate that you desire to ultimately please God and be unrestricted in the worship experience.

One day my pastor requested that we add a particular song to our set list. So I planned out a Sunday that the song would nicely be incorporated into our set. Well that service came and holy spirit absolutely came in the room during worship and we were put in a place where we had to abandon the entire setlist and allow God to move. The pastor's favorite song no longer took priority in that moment. And neither did the songs that I chose for that matter. If your leader is sensitive to the holy spirit then when you are forced to pivot due to a move of God, your leader should be understanding. Though that was just an example, there may be times where you are faced with the hard decision to do what your pastor is requesting or be obedient to God. If your pastor's ear is turned to God, the three of us should be in alignment.(God, My Pastor, and Me)

In conclusion, it's essential to maintain honor as you maneuver between your commitment to God and your respect and support for your pastor. While it's natural to want to please both, your ultimate allegiance is to God. Approach challenges with love, understanding, and wisdom, and you'll navigate the path in a way that honors both God and your pastor. God honors our obedience.

CHAPTER Six
Cont'd

Have you ever felt conflicted, where you had to choose between your pastor and God? What did you do in that instance?

_____
_____
_____
_____
_____
_____
_____
_____
_____
_____
_____
_____
_____
_____
_____
_____
_____

CHAPTER Six
Cont'd

Chapter Six
Cont'd

CHAPTER Seven

How To Handle Loss
Someone transitioning off the team

One of the realities of life is that people come and go; this principle remains true in ministry. However, we would love to have people serve alongside us for life. Unfortunately, for various reasons, you will have to deal with loss. The way you handle someone transitioning will impact the morale of the team. People may transition because they are moving out of state to go to college or because of harbored offenses. The most important thing that you can do once you are made aware of someone's intention to leave is to become a master communicator. Schedule a meeting with the individual leaving and conduct an exit interview. Ask them why they are transitioning, when they intend to stop serving, where they are transitioning to, and what you can do to ensure that this transition is smooth for them. First, you must identify the "Why". If they are leaving on positive terms (such as moving to another state or going back to school) honor them on their way out. Conduct an evaluation where you allow them to answer questions such as: How did you enjoy your time serving on the worship team? What were some positive experiences you had while serving and what were some challenging times you faced? Once you have gathered all of the information, put it in writing and email senior leadership so they are aware of the individual leaving your team.

Chapter Seven

How To Handle Loss
Someone transitioning off the team

Next, communicate with your team. Inform them that their fellow teammate is transitioning and make sure to have upbeat positive energy when sharing this news. If you share the news with discontent and an attitude the team will follow suit or be impacted by the temperature you have set concerning their departure. This will send a message to your team that this individual leaving is doing so in error. When honestly they should be shown love and support for leaving in proper order and on positive terms. This will also show the team the proper way to leave and the benefits of doing so the correct way. Consider throwing them a party with their peers, or giving them a special gift as they depart to encourage them and let them know that even though they are leaving the church, they still have a family here that cares.

Chapter Seven
Cont'd

For those on your team who are leaving in a negative way and holding onto offense, it is still important to be a master communicator. Conduct an exit interview and assess their reasons for leaving. Once they have raised concerns, address them directly. Be sober minded and leave your emotions at the door. Be objective and try to express compassion in your response, even if you disagree. If you notice that the individual is stuck in their offense and is unwilling to find common ground, offer them the option to involve a third party from senior leadership. If they refuse and have their mind made up about leaving, let them go. More than likely their inner feelings of discontent were affecting the team at some point anyways and to prevent a spread of disease, let them go. But here is the trick, still honor them on their way out. The magnitude of the celebration may be different from the person who left on good terms, but it is important to do your part in maintaining honor. Instead of throwing this individual a party, you can get a card and have the team sign it. When it comes time to communicate to your team about the departure, this meeting will be handled differently. The purpose of this meeting will be to let the team know that their teammate is leaving. Avoid sharing sensitive information or too many details, but be honest. This is a great opportunity to assess the team and do a temperature check. If one member is disgruntled, it is likely that there are more. Use this experience as a chance to learn and reflect on the reasons behind the loss and see what can be improved in team dynamics, leadership style, or organizational policies. Encourage open communication and cultivate an environment where team members feel comfortable sharing their concerns, so that potential issues can be identified and addressed before they lead to more departures.

Remember that people often leave roles for various reasons, many of which may have nothing to do with the team, leadership, or even the organization itself. Recognize your emotions and allow yourself to feel sad or upset about their departure, but make sure these feelings do not cloud your judgment or interactions.

CHAPTER Seven
Cont'd

Write down a time someone left your team. How did it make you feel? How did you handle the transition? How did your team handle the transition? Did you notice a shift in dynamics with the team after they left? What could you have done better?

_____
_____
_____
_____
_____
_____
_____
_____
_____
_____
_____
_____
_____
_____
_____
_____
_____
_____
_____
_____
_____

CHAPTER Seven
Cont'd

CHAPTER *Seven*
Cont'd

CHAPTER eight

Worship Leader vs Worship Pastor

The differences between a worship leader and a worship pastor:

I will never forget the day my Apostle said that he wanted to make me a Pastor. My first reaction was laughter because I thought it was unnecessary. Growing up I never desired to be a Pastor. I never saw that for my future and I didn't think it was an important step stone for a worship leader. But my Apostle had a vision for the worship and arts department. He knew he wanted someone to do more than run rehearsals and lead a few songs. He wanted to establish someone over the department that would be a spiritual pillar for those serving under my umbrella. He wanted me to shift my thinking and responsibilities from leading a worship experience to building, cultivating, and stewarding people. I had to shift my perspective of my team from being volunteers helping to accomplish the big goal to being souls and sheep that needed tending and spiritual guidance. I want to make clear that you don't have to have the title "Pastor" to pray, encourage, and give spiritual guidance to your team. But I do want to acknowledge the power and weight of having the title and what expectations come with the role of being a worship pastor.

As a worship pastor you now become a multidimensional leader that must be sensitive to the burdens and spiritual health of those that serve on your team. Now when you give correction, it is no longer just because someone is running late, but you are now challenging your team to live a life of purity and assessing just that sometimes. You are also now obligated to pray and fast and challenge them on a spiritual level. This starts by getting to know your team on a deeper level.

CHAPTER eight
Cont'd

Worship Leader vs Worship Pastor

There were many times throughout my time as a worship leader and worship pastor that I had to step up for my team in a serious way. Whether it was a team member dealing with cancer, losing a close loved one, becoming homeless, dealing with suicide attempts, struggling with their lifestyle choices, having to sing at funerals and make hospital visits, and more. Your ability to guide, redirect, cover, and protect your team is what makes you a master gatekeeper and leader. Additionally, your ability to steward and cultivate ones gift is also what makes you an impactful worship pastor. Your senior leaders may not be ready to give you the title pastor yet, but there are things you can do now to show extra care and attention to those you serve alongside. Firstly, check-in on your team, be intentional to ask them nothing about worship. Ask them about their personal life, work life, and relationships. Ask them what are some things that are a current burden for them, and what is something they do outside of ministry that brings them joy.

As they begin to share, never take on a judgmental tone. Always show compassion and understanding towards where a person currently is in this season of their life. Although, as their leader you should always guide them and challenge them to do better. The reality is that while you are holding their arms up in this season, you may also still be dealing with your own personal attacks. Imagine praying and believing God for the healing of your team member's body while you are still waiting for your own healing. This is how selfless you must become.

However, as worship pastors we must use discernment and wisdom to know when we may have to ask a team member to sit down from serving for a season until they recover, heal, break ties with whatever has them bound, ect. We must be accountable with our leaders while making these decisions, but the reality is that some people will not sit themselves down. So you will have to make the best decision for their spiritual health and the health of your team.

As leaders we must constantly asses and evaluate the health of our team by walking closely with those that we serve among.

CHAPTER eight
Cont'd

Challenge:

Write down a list of each member of your team, beside their name, list their areas of growth. List ways that they are an asset, your growth plan for them, and how you can celebrate their wins.

Example:

Terry Johnson: (Alto) - Member for 1 year.

Assets: Vocally strong and consistent alto. They have a positive attitude and remain teachable.

Areas of Growth: Consistently late. Struggles to keep up during prophetic moments. She needs ear training.

Growth Plan: Ensure that she spends more time during rehearsal flowing prophetically. Do vocal exercises that will strengthen her ear. Have an honest conversation about her tardiness and your expectations for the team.

Celebrate Wins: I will verbally encourage Terry more often. I will show her appreciation for being a consistent alto with a positive attitude while still challenging her to be on time and to grow vocally.

CHAPTER *eight*
Cont'd

Name

_____
_____
_____
_____

Assets

_____
_____
_____
_____

Areas of Growth

_____
_____
_____
_____

Growth Plan

_____
_____
_____
_____
_____

CHAPTER eight
Cont'd

Name

Assets

Areas of Growth

Growth Plan

CHAPTER *eight*
Cont'd

Name
___
___
___

Assets
___
___
___

Areas of Growth
___
___
___

Growth Plan
___
___
___
___

CHAPTER *eight*
Cont'd

Name

Assets

Areas of Growth

Growth Plan

CHAPTER eight
Cont'd

Name
_____
_____
_____
_____
_____

Assets
_____
_____
_____
_____
_____

Areas of Growth
_____
_____
_____
_____

Growth Plan
_____
_____
_____
_____
_____
_____

CHAPTER eight
Cont'd

Name

_____
_____
_____

Assets

_____
_____
_____
_____

Areas of Growth

_____
_____
_____
_____

Growth Plan

_____
_____
_____
_____
_____
_____
_____

CHAPTER eight
Cont'd

Name
_____
_____
_____
_____

Assets
_____
_____
_____
_____

Areas of Growth
_____
_____
_____
_____

Growth Plan
_____
_____
_____
_____
_____
_____

CHAPTER *eight*
Cont'd

Name

Assets

Areas of Growth

Growth Plan

CHAPTER eight *Cont'd*

Name

_____
_____
_____
_____

Assets

_____
_____
_____
_____

Areas of Growth

_____
_____
_____
_____

Growth Plan

_____
_____
_____
_____
_____

CHAPTER *eight*
Cont'd

Name

_____
_____
_____
_____

Assets

_____
_____
_____
_____

Areas of Growth

_____
_____
_____
_____

Growth Plan

_____
_____
_____
_____
_____
_____

CHAPTER *eight*
Cont'd

Name
___
___
___
___

Assets
___
___
___
___

Areas of Growth
___
___
___
___

Growth Plan
___
___
___
___
___

CHAPTER nine

How to balance ministry and your personal life

Let's talk about death. Here's a hard truth: One day, we are all going to die. When I reflect on my life, I want to feel a sense of fulfillment. I want to be able to say that I lived a good life and pleased God. I want God to be proud of my "Yes" and commitment to His assignment. But I also want to be able to say that I enjoyed my life. Have you ever considered what would happen if you died today? A hard pill to swallow is that life would go on. Yes, there would be tears and mourning. Yes, people would be sad and devastated. But eventually, they would hire another worship leader to take your place. I know this fact is painful to process but I say all this to emphasize that when you need a day or even a week for yourself, take it! The number of pastors resigning from their positions or even resorting to suicide due to their inability to take a break has significantly increased. Though many people in ministry are quitting for various reasons. I believe that if we were able to schedule more breaks and prioritize mental health days, we would have more healthy and strong leaders.

CHAPTER *nine*

How to balance ministry and your personal life

This chapter is for the worship leader who struggles to take time off for themselves. They feel as though if they miss a Sunday, the service would fail. They may even fear being replaced, and no longer needed if they don't show up. This is a sign of idolatry and a lack of preparation. Your ability to prepare your church for your absence is a sign of security and maturity. When they have a successful service without you there, that is still a good reflection of you. Finding the balance between ministry and your personal life is crucial for your mental, physical, and emotional well being. The decision to find balance in ministry is detrimental to your longevity as a worship leader. Yes, we should be willing to lay down our lives for Him like Christ did for us, but we should not kill ourselves in the process. Spiritual death and physical death are two different things. I want my spirit man to die daily so that I can continue to do the work of the Lord, but my physical body must remain strong. Finding time to do something for yourself is important. Whether it's taking a family vacation, going to the spa, or even finding a conference to attend in order to be poured into spiritually; you must prioritize your own well being. Your ability to serve in ministry for 50 years or more will be marked by your unrestricted "yes" to God and your wisdom in caring for your personal health.

CHAPTER *nine*

How to balance ministry and your personal life

Lets talk about our physical health. Unfortunately, the gospel community is the only community that glorifies obesity, whereas traditionally secular artists are expected to be small, petite, and physically fit. However, the Christian world does not hold the same standards. While I am thrilled that we are more accepting and inclusive, I am concerned about what that means for our endurance and longevity in this kingdom business. Now, before anyone gets offended, let me be the first to say that I am a plus sized woman who has struggled with my weight over the years, so there is no judgment here. In fact, I speak from personal experience when I say that I know being out of shape can hinder your ability to minister effectively. Truth be told, size doesn't always determine you being in shape. There are plenty of petite people running out of breath while they lead worship. This is a call and challenge for all of us to prioritize our physical health by going to the gym and eating healthy, so that we can increase our endurance in worship. I know what it's like to desire to jump and run around the stage, and feeling limited in what you can do. However, making good choices one day at a time can have a life-altering effect.

When was the last time you went to therapy? The altar and counselors are both necessary. After you have cried out at the altar and found freedom, don't hesitate to seek professional Christian counselors that can help you break down the patterns of your addictions and strongholds. They can provide you with tools to prevent you from going back to the things that you have just released. I can personally attest that finding counselors who can help you break things down and offer a healthy perspective, even challenging your behaviors, is a beneficial decision.

CHAPTER *nine*

How to balance ministry and your personal life

Finding balance as a worship leader also means balancing your family, friendships, personal businesses, and ministry. You may have heard the saying, "family is your first ministry," but we all know how challenging that can truly be. When I met my husband, I was already fully immersed in ministry. I didn't always have the wisdom to prioritize my husband over ministry. Although he is low maintenance and very understanding of my assignment, it is important to find that balance and understand that your spouse and children still need you to function in your role as a mother and wife at home; this is vital. While they respect your title at church, your family is the only group of people that need you to leave that at the door and become a provider, protector, nurturer, and keeper of the home.

So be a good steward of the assignment and title, but also be a good steward of yourself. Find the balance. Learn how to slay giants, and enjoy time with your friends and family. Learn how to cast demons out, and go to the beach and collect seashells. Learn how to open the heavens, and enjoy a good comedy show on your day off. Live a little! The only people that want you to lock yourself away until it's time to minister are the religious ones! Your deserve to be full of joy in every area of your life. We will no longer settle for thriving ministries and miserable marriages, or a successful worship service and a lack of good friends around you. Let peace and joy be your portion.

CHAPTER *nine*

How to balance ministry and your personal life

WRITE DOWN A LIST OF THINGS YOU CAN DO TO FIND BALANCE:

_____
_____
_____
_____
_____
_____
_____
_____
_____
_____
_____
_____
_____

CHAPTER nine

How to balance ministry and your personal life

CHAPTER nine

How to balance ministry and your personal life

CHAPTER Ten

The Humanity of a Worship Leader

I was born into a family already operating in ministry. So I never had the opportunity to choose God for myself. Well, obviously I had to eventually grow up and make a decision of my own, but I was never presented with buddhism, the muslim faith, or even atheism. I was forced to spend time with a man named Jesus since the time I was born. I experienced religion before I had a relationship with God. I knew church-isms before I fully understood who God was. Though I am grateful that my parents kept me surrounded by believers, I still dealt with real life struggles. I experienced sexual abuse from family friends at an early age, and battled with perversion and my identity. I was the 17 year old girl in a 21 and up club with a fake I.D. I was the 17 year old at college frat parties drunk and high being carried out by men I didn't know on a saturday night. But guess where I always made it on time to Sunday morning, Church. Though I was just a teenager going through the normal phases of life, I was always torn because I had also begun to develop a relationship with God. I could not deny the encounters I was having in the presence of the Lord, but my flesh still desired the things of the world. So as I matured and continued to walk with God my convictions grew but for whatever reason, I struggled to break the cycle of sin.

CHAPTER Ten

The Humanity of a Worship Leader

So what do you do when your gifting exceeds your ability to live right? What do you do when you're experiencing growth and advancement in ministry but you haven't fully gained control of your flesh? The truth is, most people conceal their struggles to avoid judgment, accountability, or feel that they are unworthy of the call. However, it is important to remember that regardless of what people see, God sees us. And honestly, sin has a way of rearing its head and exposing us in one way or the other. So what do you do when you're making an impact at church, witnessing souls being saved but going home and dying spiritually as you wrestle with your flesh? This is the situation I faced when I discovered I was pregnant while serving as the worship pastor of a prominent church in Atlanta. I was devastated because my flesh almost sabotaged the call of God on my life. My lack of self control almost cost me everything. The shame and guilt that came along with the harsh reality that I had disappointed everyone that believed in me; my team, my leaders, and the congregation. How do you lead a team of people, and place an expectation on them when you have yet to slay the giant in your own life? How can you challenge your team to live a pure and holy life when you as their leader are struggling? These were all of the thoughts that ran through my head.

CHAPTER Ten

The Humanity of a Worship Leader

One of the hardest things I had to do was to tell my spiritual covering and my team that I had let them down. What happened next you might ask? My pastors covered me. They prayed for me and came up with a plan to inform the team. They corrected me but also loved on me. As a consequence of my decision, I spent six months sitting on the front row unable to lead worship. I almost destroyed me.(read that last line again) I had no one to blame but myself. During my pregnancy, I was mostly depressed and angry with myself, despite the love and support I received from my church family. They threw me a baby shower, a gender reveal, and visited me and my son at the hospital. It took me years to recover mentally, vocally, physically, and emotionally, and it took time to forgive myself. My insecurity was at an all time high afterwards because I didn't know how my team or congregation would receive from me after my fall. However, I have discovered that there is glory after a fall.

One particular Sunday, without warning, my pastor called me on stage while I was pregnant and told the whole church that I was still his daughter in whom he was well pleased. That this mistake would not be the end of me. That he had my back and he and his wife would be loving on me and supporting me throughout this journey and that I am still anointed and still worthy of the call. I was blown away. I had never witnessed such an act and acceptance before in my life! He could have kicked me out of his church, hid me away, or been ashamed, but instead he insisted that I sit on the front row every Sunday. He refused to let me shy away and hide in the back. After counseling and spending some time away with my child, he restored me back into my position as the worship pastor. I want to emphasize again that I have never seen this kind of restoration before in ministry, but I am so incredibly grateful that it happened to me. That I was able to experience genuine love, forgiveness, and restoration. My team embraced me with love and were excited to have me back. I was able to minister to them from a place of vulnerability and transparency. They were able to witness the love of God through my mistakes. I spent time rebuilding trust with my team and using my life as a testimony to the grace of God as well as the reality of falling from a place of authority.

CHAPTER Ten

The Humanity of a Worship Leader

Have you ever struggled with sin while in a position of leadership? Who were you accountable with? What are you doing to break cycles of sin?

_____
_____
_____
_____
_____
_____
_____
_____
_____
_____
_____
_____
_____
_____
_____
_____

CHAPTER Ten

The Humanity of a Worship Leader

BONUS CHAPTER

Armorbearers
Yes or No?

I remember the day when I had just finished ministering at a three-day conference. I was completely exhausted. The entire team sat on the side of the stage, frozen and unable to move because of how sore our bodies were. We sat there, physically depleted, catching our breath before having to make a long walk to our cars parked at the very back of the church. It was at this moment when a young lady walked up to me and asked if she could pray for me. I was familiar with her, but alarm bells went off in my head because she wasn't someone I trusted to pray for me. She had been in a season where she was in and out of the church, dealing with life, and was not in the best spiritual condition to pray for me. Yet there she was asking me in front of my team if she could pray for my feet! Yes, she wanted to lay hands on my feet. And because of my desire to not embarrass her, I allowed her to. Yeah, I know what you are thinking. I should have told her no and politely excused her, but I didn't. Just like some victims of sexual assault who allow their abusers to get away for fear of causing an uproar, the cycle repeated itself during a simple request of prayer. You might be wondering, what is the big deal? Why shouldn't we allow everyone to pray for us? Well, time would reveal that she operates in witchcraft and reads tarot cards and does palm readings. Yes, I allowed her to pray and lay hands on my feet. I didn't know about her practices at the time, but my discernment was telling me that she wasn't someone I should have allowed to lay hands on me. That's when I realized that I needed an armor bearer.

BONUS CHAPTER

Armorbearers Yes or No?

I get it. You don't want to seem crazy. If you're anything like me, you don't want to draw unnecessary attention to yourself. You feel that walking with an armor bearer might make people think you are trying to be a celebrity in the church, or trying to be grand. Trust me, I understand. However you need to realize that what you carry is sacred and must be protected at all costs. Now, you need to discern what season you're in. I went years without one and for the most part, I was fine. But there came a time when I needed someone to walk with me, provide relief in certain ministry areas, pray, and cover me. The most important thing to remember is that even though you have someone guarding you, your prayer life must still remain strong. You must not let your guard down because you have obtained an armor bearer. The truth is, this individual is a human being with a soul just like everyone else. There will be times when your armor bearer needs you to pour into them, just like everyone else. A mature armor bearer will be sensitive as to when to pull on you.

BONUS CHAPTER

Armorbearers Yes or No?

I remember attending a ministry assignment by myself. (This was my first problem!) As I am sitting on the front row, a man walks from the other side of the church and lays his hand on my chest to pray. The keywords that should stick out from that last sentence are "Man" and "My Chest". Unacceptable is the only word that comes to mind. I immediately removed his hand and firmly told him "No". This situation once again highlights the importance of having someone who can speak up on your behalf. It is crucial for you to maintain a positive image and keep your reputation untarnished so that when it is time to minister, the congregation can receive from you without the stains of offense. While it is sometimes unavoidable, an armor bearer can act as a barrier between you and the difficult conversations that need to be had with people. However, it is important to remember to never allow your armor bearer to come between you and your team. Your team must have a healthy amount of access to you. I always maintain an open-door policy with my team because they are the closest people to me during worship. This relationship must remain genuine and pure. Allowing your armor bearer to create distance between you and your team can cause division, frustration, and offense.

When you decide to have an armor bearer, it is important to ensure that you are accountable to your pastor. You never want to establish a new norm for one of their members, without them being aware. It is also important to remember that this individual serving you is God's servant first, your pastors sheep second, and then your armor bearer third. You must use wisdom to ensure that boundaries are set and abuse of their service to you is never an occurrence.

Do you believe an armor bearer is necessary for you? Why or why not? What can you do to ensure that you are covered while on ministry assignments?

The Worship Leader's MANUAL
A GUIDE TO A HEALTHY AND IMPACTFUL WORSHIP TEAM

This Manual is a tool for worship leaders to help establish and develop an impactful team. You will get information on how to onboard team members, develop them spiritually, how to deal with conflict, how to carry the vision of your senior leaders, how to balance your personal life and your assignment and much more! I pray this book gives you the jump start you need to revamp your ministry for your local assembly. This book is intended to be paired with "The Workbook"- An Interactive Study Guide for Worship Teams.

As you read the manual, your team should be reading the workbook. Purchase both books so you can lead your team into the many activities provided for them.

Anna has lead worship at Embassy City Church under Apostle Bryan Meadows and Patrice Meadows since 2011. Pastor Anna's voice carries a unique sound that captivates congregations and a vibrant personality that evokes security in the faith of other believers.

Pastor Anna's music is both beautifully orchestrated and prophetically positioned to shift the atmosphere wherever it is released and unravels generational bondage off God's people.

She found passion in developing worship leader's from all over the world through her mentorship group "Worship Leader's Unite" and has created training and development tracts for worship leaders and their teams. She desires to see worship ministries whole and thriving through unity, aligned vision, and spiritual maturity.

In 2018, God led Pastor Anna to share her testimony of trial and triumph on her journey to accepting her call, in her first published book "From Glory to Grace: The Story of a Rose" which is available on Amazon.

Pastor Anna is a devoted wife to her husband Robert and together they have a beautiful son, Arrow.

@ANNALONELLE :IG

Made in the USA
Columbia, SC
01 February 2024

31303860R00046